Writing King Kong

Yet all experience is an arch, wherethro'
gleams that untravell'd world, whose margin fades
for ever and for ever when I move
  — Alfred, Lord Tennyson, *Ulysses*

Writing King Kong
Robert Seatter

SEREN

Seren is the book imprint of
Poetry Wales Press Ltd.
57 Nolton Street, Bridgend, Wales, CF31 3AE
Visit our new website! www.serenbooks.com

ISBN: 978-1-85411-545-4

A CIP record for this title is available from the British Library.

The publisher acknowledges the financial assistance of the Welsh Books Council.

Cover image: Getty Images

Printed in Bembo by The Berforts Group Ltd, Stevenage

Contents

Writing *King Kong*

Why does he make a detour to tear down the elevated railway on 3rd Avenue?
Because Cooper, writer and director of King Kong, had once lived beside the
tracks and resented the way the clatter of the trains kept him awake.
                                        – Peter Conrad, *The Observer*

It's where I stop in my daily walk,
at the corner of 5th Avenue, 33rd and 34th St.,
budge that obstacle against my daily sun,
blink away its shadow. The Empire State Building –
just a giant toy, a large crick in my neck.
A version of that ceaseless night train
clattering along its broken tracks… another train,
another robbed and sleepless hour.
All the things that elude me stay in my mind,
stick to my pen. Love given is forgotten, a bed I lie on
to dream my dreams of somewhere else,
but that girl in the penthouse, on Hollywood Blvd.,
with her faraway small teeth that make her
faraway perfect smile, sharp as a photograph,
I could carry forever in my suit breast pocket;
that elusive novel inscribed with gold letters,
'Merian C. Cooper' along its spine,
which waits in the bookstore on 33rd East, 17th St.,
it never flickers out inside the dark;
or that sleep of mine….

So I'll move his black arms to open the latch
of her doll's house window,
push the tallest tower into a puff of dust,
or – before that – make this detour
to twitch the train off its airfix bridge.
Now there's sleep and sky and her perfect smile
for me. Could I write it any better?

Six Million Hand-driven Rivets

My father is dying – tentatively, unhappily –
and I give him a bridge.

Precisely, I give him Sydney Harbour Bridge,
this Christmas, this turning year,

as I travel under it, gazing up at all its iron.
Girder-strong, massive, the old world built this

into the new. There are photos of Englishmen
in 1930 in waistcoats and cufflinks

and neat bowties, straddling the sky, hammering
rivets into air. My father would approve:

How many rivets? he'd ask me.
Facts, hard facts. I'd tell him the answers

to ease the time – and the number of man hours,
the number of years, before they could journey

over the water with perfect confidence,
step on step, to reach the other side.

Party Line

Back then we all had one –
in the 60s, perhaps even as late as the 70s.
My parents used it as an excuse
for people they didn't want to phone.
We got the party line, they'd say, *couldn't get through.*
It was someone else's voice
coming down your black receiver,
or else, more strange and interesting,
it was someone else's conversation,
all their intimate to and fro, that you walked right into
without a word of introduction.
And there you'd sit quiet, an accidental spy,
eavesdropping into another life
till one of them said, slightly quizzical, then slightly cross,
I think there's someone on the party line.
But by then it was too late –
you had slipped imperceptibly into their lives.
For a minute you were there, in a different house;
your shoes felt different, even the tie
around your neck, the weight on your toes,
and someone unknown was telling you everything,
tipping their story into your ear,
and you were nodding back to them there in the dark.
It was what you'd always wanted,
just for a moment: a different identity slid into
like a new shiny skin, with a different pair
of ears and eyes. Even a different street
to walk out into the night –
where you'd wonder what advice,
what consolation, what last intimate word
you might offer up to them
if ever they rang you again.

21 Ways of Starting a New Life

It's like putting up a tent, or that tricky moment
with a deckchair. Belief is all.

Just imagine now you're lying there –
sunslicked, warm. Or safe under that canopy,

rain tick-ticking on its slope of canvas.
It's just another foreign ceiling.

Or it's like speaking Japanese –
what you'd always wanted.

That's you in dark glasses, skin smooth as rice,
undoing words like sushi parcels.

Easy as taste. Red words, green words,
a long yellow syllable. Fish or fowl?

And in the Year of the Pig, if you were an animal,
what would you be?

It's just becoming the game.
But not the torture of party games.

Breathe a new body, new eyes, new hair.
Imagination is all.

Take wings. Take instructions.
Take hope. Take prayer.

A Buddha on a keyring. A de-sanctified St Christopher.
A sleek black cat. A silver spoon. Significance is all.

It's what you are, and what you wanted to be.
The dots of brightness out there in the dark –

aren't they the same as the ones before?
Persistence is all.

Or that tiny station when you look backwards
from the train, wasn't that you there?

Not passing but waving, not waving
but passing. Perspective is all.

Or it's like losing your way to the house
where you live, and discovering a new street.

The chimney pot you never noticed
which shifts the skyline. Detail is all.

Or a ritual of coffee cups in an unknown bar
on the long road to Ithaca.

That clock's familiar. But not the face in that mirror.
You're in a different film, another story.

But that next coffee cup is quite believable,
and you're breathing quite calmly.

This is not a deckchair, not even a tent.
Just another way of starting. Belief is all.

Translating Chekhov in Tennis Whites

from a line of a poem by Robert Hass

He was translating Chekhov and wore tennis whites.
Why should he make me laugh?

Fastidious perfection in dress, repose in sunlight,
that was so Chekhovian. Slipping into

first the body, the seated pose, the head and neck
incline of the man, then bit by bit

into his mind. Ticking like a neat machine,
picking words and holding them

up to that sunlight, working at it through the slow,
sloping hours. Then later in the night,

hearing their voices saying the words, *his* words now –
as he lay bereft of tennis whites,

naked and uncertain – their mouths defined
for a moment, then rubbed out

into the corners of the room. *That would never do,*
he'd say. They had eluded him again.

So hard, this meeting himself, not quite
meeting himself, in others' words.

As a child, he had cried at the thought of never ever
really knowing another human soul. Now

he wore tennis whites, shrugged on, off
all their unknowing, held his breath

somewhere in between.

Je m'appelle

I say the words to the mirror
in this white-walled room.
Je m'appelle Robert. Before I go out

down the long wooden corridor.
Breakfast is waiting. *Petit dejeuner.*
Maman et papa. La famille.
Le chien which does not like me.
Breakfast bowls make a different sound
from English cups and saucers,
spill all the words. Doors slam
differently too. *Au revoir –*

j'ai quatorze ans et je viens de l'Angleterre.
Outside everyone's speaking
in high-pitched sounds: up and down
birds on loops of telegraph wire.
High skimmers flying in and out
of clouds. Doing it on purpose.
I copy them in my head,

then up there on *la Tour Eiffel,*
I make them very small and silent,
so I am king of all the world's noise.
Yes, I am the roaring boy. *Oui, mais oui.*
And I laugh out loud at all the jokes
I could tell, if I chose.

Pip

She took up the candle. We went up one staircase and then another.
More passages and up another staircase, and only the candle lighted us.
— Charles Dickens, *Great Expectations*

Class is the stairway, and I
climb it. In my thick brown boots,
with my coarse red hands

on the balustrade.
To the light at the top,
which is beauty, the girl,

the other. Her unkissable cheek,
her middle-distance gaze.
That somewhere else life,

which I write in the night,
on my tight, folded sheet, on my window square,
on the long, worn planks of wooden floor.

My own spacious story.
Now I reach to touch, but class
is the stairway, and down it I go.

She points me down, she beggars me
again. Cards on the table, upside down
hearts. Her middle distance gaze.

Time is the room. The woman in white,
the lost shoe, the lost years.
And all the things I can never understand

are muddled on the table.
What do I touch here, Pip? she asks.
The heart, I reply. But what is the heart?

What we learn on the journey
from water to land, from the cold marsh country
to the red of fire. All the up and down

stairways. The desire in the distance.
The strange distance of desire.
And I climb, still I climb.

O

It's that bit at the end of *The English Patient*
where he carries her body out of the cave.
His mouth a huge O of pain.

A sandblown, unshaven Ralph Fiennes.
A dead but beautiful Kristin Scott Thomas.
And we revisit the whole story. How they got there –

the shadow of their aeroplane over that caramel desert,
the yards and yards of her impossibly long, billowing
white scarf. Then their words of love

in those ridiculous, over-clipped accents,
his face on the pillow in its burnt, puckered mask –
how many hours and hours of prosthetics?

But in spite of it all, it's that O that stays with us.
Unattainable. Such love, such grief too.
And behind him, that vast, dark mouth of the cave.

And where are we? We're outside the cave,
stuttering, distracted. By flies, by headaches, by heat.
By how to begin. O O O. We cannot even begin.

On not Dreaming

Though of course I do, don't I?
I know the stats: the rapid eye movements
repeating in cycles every 90 minutes,

the 40-minute dreamscape that comes on the point
just before waking, the 27 years
of all my life that some busy statistician has calculated

I shall spend in dreaming. And the tiredness I feel now,
as morning smacks the window, the blind, the square
of carpet, tells me that something has been going on.

There's a dent in the pillow to the side of my head.
There's a dusty cloud in the bedroom air. There's
a dumb other self that's eloquent, all-knowing,

who goes walking around me all day long
in rubber-soled shoes that gently squeak.
He prods me, questions me, whistles a thin, cool breath

into my ear, takes the slow echo that comes
travelling back. Then looks at me teasingly
as if to say: *So that's what you really think, is it?*

The Dream of the Changing Shirts

You're ranging the house, room after
room, in a shirt of mustard yellow, now

dark red, now lime green, now cobalt
blue against the blue wall;

you're disappearing into the upper rooms
down darkening corridors and I

follow you, how I follow –
catching at detail: your purple cuff, indigo

blue shirt tail, one green button –
round doors, in mirrors, to the top

of the stair, curious for the next
changing colour, and hopeful of course

for more: the sweat of you
on cotton, on linen, a trace

of your blood – some shaving cut?
rusty on a collar, even perhaps at the last

your heart unbuttoned – another button,
another... but no, there's still

too much night and you're off again:
a cinnamon sleeve at a door handle,

now charcoal grey, now magenta,
and I follow you, how I follow

Sleep

We make our hotel room the shape of it,
through days of constant rain:

bad wallpaper, blind, light bulb candelabra,
a blank TV screen and pocked net curtaining.

We demand extra blankets of it in coarse beige wool
from the hard-faced receptionist.

Merci Madame, merci de rien.
Our lips have closed before they've opened.

Then we rub our fingertips across its texture
of creased, week-old newspapers, half-read novels,

chalky talcum powder, and one dusty sock
found under the bed.

As if we had stored it up
from late nights at the office, the days, the years

of bus stops, tube stops, horizon myopia,
and now we unroll it, breathe it in,

lie in its drunk and dirty corners
among the cat fleas, the spiders,

the slow drift of skin flakes,
inside that so unfamiliar smell of ourselves.

My Father Tells Me His Dreams

How he's in New York, a city he's never been to,
and he's 50 years old not 85,
searching for a hotel, a cheap hotel;
how he can't find one,

and every expensive hotel he goes to,
they rob him – so at last, arriving at a suitable hotel,
my father tells them he cannot pay.
For look, I've no money, that's what your city has done to me.

No matter, they say, *we see what our city
has done to you, and so you can stay.*
It doesn't make sense, my father tells me, shaking his head.
No, it doesn't make sense, I agree,

and for the first time for a long time,
we're here together
in this place that doesn't make sense.
After a long journey,

it's the surprise of a small, warm room,
where his tattered suit lies
carefully folded on a chair,
where we sit together wondering in the silence.

Singing Hymns with Jean

for Jean Sprackland

After too much red wine and vegetarian lasagne,
we begin. *You go first. No, you.* Will it be a defiant rally
of 'My Song is Love Unknown', or something funereal,
'Jesu, Lover of My Soul', where I do organ rolls
with my fingers on the kitchen wooden table?

It's not belief, for we have both lost that
many years ago. Perhaps it's a sense of togetherness,
partly I suppose what hymns were invented for.
Or merely perhaps a raucous desire to sing.
And did those feet in ancient time, walk upon....

Whatever it is, for a moment we are back there,
in the school assembly – that vast parquet floor –
distracted by sex and undone homework.
Yet opening our mouths like automata toys,
Onward Christian soldiers marching as to war,

we crisp the consonants. Or in the dim light
of a suburban church, I paddle the melody
of 'The Day Thou Gavest, Lord has Ended',
count the slow minutes as the big church chills.
It was the language too we loved. *No hobgoblin*

nor foul fiend – how evil made a crusty sound.
His first avowed intent to be a pilgrim – how goodness
sounded so beautifully clear, a simple infinitive
floating on the air. And how loneliness was *that green hill faraway,*
sad to be wall-less though we never knew why.

But I know we'll end with 'Hills of the North',
for which you, being Northern, can claim some ownership.
Your hills and rocks, my southern caves –
pent be each warring breeze. This was our geography,
out of time, out of sync even then.

Shout while you journey home – we sing the last verse
in a hoarse crescendo. We know we'll never get back there,
but – pass the red wine – we still sing.
Yes, perhaps that's why we sing.

Fred & Ginger

every bone in
your leg her leg
your back her back
click clack tick tack
facing the music
there may be trouble ahead
but tarsus metatarsus
meta meta tarsus
can I x-ray this joy?
I have found a new purpose
for stairways lampposts
hats and umbrellas
I have found a new
clack tack
stack the vertebrae
up cup up cup
meta meta tarsus
can I x-ray this x-ray?
the heart a cloud rising
the joy of all surfaces
change partners and dance with
all the rooms full
the bowls overflowing
dear Fred dear Ginger
those black & white Saturdays
before the fiddlers have fled
are fleeing will flee
this arm to arm melting
your face my face
inside the mirror
click to click
clack to clack
this to this joy

Bank Holiday

Sara, my Italian neighbour, has pink curlers in her hair
which mean a night on the town or a Catholic feastday.
I watch her in the garden below my balcony,

chopping nuts, slicing beans on the table all morning,
her voice hello-ing up to me through the trellis of ivy.
And soon the guests will come –

men with their dark coffee laughter,
the girlfriends of the sons with almond-shaped eyes,
all the easy sounds of their coming and going

floating up to my balcony. Later, perhaps a barbecue,
slow drift of smoke through the branches of my plum tree,
their voices the other side of my hedge in the night.

You are always somewhere else these Bank Holiday days:
working for double pay, sorting out your room,
moving the heaps of paper from one corner to another,

or sitting on your balcony watching the plane tree.
Yet we are always storing it up out of interminable routine,
our perfect bank holiday. I can see it quite clearly:

there's a balcony, a table, the first strawberries of the season –
you brought them in a cardboard punnet,
sliced them into soft red halves,

sprinkled them with caster sugar.
They shine and glitter in their bowls in the sun –
always just out of reach.

Pizza

'Quattro stagione' are too many for you, or never enough.
And destinations from New York to Venice
leave you mapless in the restaurant, a half-mouthful
of mozzarella, basil, pinenuts, a craving now
for pepperoni, hot sausage, pancetta, a drizzle of olive oil.
A mountain too far or an eclipsed horizon. I loved, now I love.
Then you're twitched into the newfangled –
flirting with 'our chef's new creations':
artichoke and radicchio, spicy chicken, Hawaian pineapple,
before returning again to plain Margherita
at the top of the menu. *I'll just check there's nothing
I might have missed.* That taste of opportunity....

And even when the agony of your choosing is over –
Well, that's done, I think… and it comes:
a sunset egg on a spinach sea, all dotted with capers,
you pause your expectation, swivel your head.
Choose, chose, chosen. All the white plates are spinning
in the air, all the good times are somehow wrong,
the longed-for appetites charged with uncertainty.
Now a whiff of anchovies from behind my head
has you turning to me – *You, you that I chose?* –
with an uncertain, a wondering look in your eye.

Gifts

From my journeys I bring him back
an iron lantern, a green hat with a feather,

fine leather gloves, and a book of Indian stories
which he puts by his bed but never reads.

And I bring him too this street of shoes,
where I buy hiking boots and flip flops,

maps and strong coffee; a path up
the mountain, breath-stopping, heartless.

Or this tree at the river bend, a bright red sugar maple
waving like a flag, beckoning me on.

Later, will come fruits from morning markets,
plucked from the hubbub, the clattering, the glare –

kumquat, sugar apple, star fruit, sweet tamarind.
Things he's never tasted: untongued, unswallowed.

Then I'll bring him jugs and bowls, both patterned
and plain, the hands that made them,

eyes that watched them heat and cool.
Inside, the gift of sour green water

from a forgotten well, the long horizon
of stagnant canal with its shadow

of winding gear. And at the last,
the wide, grey river to flow and flow away.

Another City

after The City *by* C.P. *Cavafy*

Why – when you have
your two-bedroom flat,
a view over London
(from the kitchen window),
your black and white artworks
crated over from Brazil
up on your living room wall,
your grandfather's watch,
fluency in three,
no four foreign languages
(all those books, all those
'listen & repeat' audio CDs),
a poem of mine in a frame,
my three telephone numbers in your mobile
for constant availability,
my shirtless body (and all the rest)
– do you stand up suddenly
in the middle of a non-birthday,
birthday dinner
(no candles, no cake, I promise,
not after the last time)
and look through
your kitchen window,
not at the view over London
but half-way
to the darkening pine trees
at the end of the basement flat garden,
and say *I'll get rid of this flat*
and go to another city?

And I look out
past your shoulder
and see quite clearly
all your rooms to come
in all your changing flats,
city after city after city,
in all your unchanging darkness.

Rhapsody in Blue

I frequently hear music in the very heart of the noise.
                                        – George Gershwin

You are all my cities, contrapuntal, busy,
interrupted. Chameleon spaces

from the opening *glissando*. Look up, it's smoke,
it's gone. *Agitato*.

And a life that comes and comes through doorways,
down tarmac, in and out

of car doors, a train
through the night, and leaping, leaping

across this Tuesday skyline. Tune chasing tune,
up and down the scale.

Step on the major, step on the minor.
Or improvise tomorrow –

I was always too serious –
to stride piano, novelty piano, any comic piano,

then play it again from a hard luck corner,
but how many times more?

I was always too much the believer.
Song from a backstreet which is loud

for a second, then muffled, gone.
Agitato e misterioso.

And I go searching, searching
all my cities

for that ache, that remembrance –
modulation through the circle of fifths –

for the way my spaces once seemed so filled.
That lost G Major.

The Owl & the Pussycat
or too much thinking on too much happiness

One day you will tire of me sang the owl to a small guitar.
Feather to fur, hard beak to soft whiskered face.

What it is to be lucky in temperament, easy to love
mused the pussycat in a moment of quite atypical philosophising.

The owl at the tiller stared ahead: what it is to be me!
A pea-green boat is a fanciful colour, the money is my worry –

the honey running out, the money, the money.
Rock-a-bye, rock-a-bye purred the pussycat.

One day we shall drown thought the owl,
down, down to an ink-dark depression: the howl of an owl.

He had planned the voyage, pre-counted bong trees;
insured their wedding day against acts of God.

So, impulse, emotion, a purple sky, they had sailed away.
A spark in his brain had said this time or never!

But after never, what then, what then?
sang the owl to his small guitar.

Let us be married purred the pussycat,
knowing full well that such was her role:

the velvet fur paw that caresses the moment,
the runcible spoon forever half-full.

In sad winter months, she'd turn on the radio:
dance with me, dance with me, by the light of the moon.

As if remembering brief happiness can make it last
sang the owl to a small guitar.

Carte Blanche

Now there's no desiring you
I sit in street cafés at tables
with a blank sheet of paper.
The trees are just trees, the cars

are just cars, and all the city goes on,
with no need at all to tell you it.
Now there's no desiring you,
at night, the sky is empty of all longing –

it is simply dark, very distant, full
of stars. And morning will break –
with a certain number of hours
all of which need to be planned for.

Now there's no desiring you,
there is just so much time
to fill up and up with unlonging,
which is blank, quite blank, and free.

Marilyn at Tracey's

a tribute to 'Marilyn in Acton, USA', *The Edward Weston Collection*

She's leaning out of a white sports car, hanging over
the driver's door – the last photos of her,

black and white, on the wall of a West London café –
windblown glamour, breezy, on the road to somewhere.

And she'd just pulled in here, Acton – only this was
a side street off the M4 to nowhere, not Acton USA –

for the local special: two eggs, bacon, black pudding and bubble.
Bubble? I can hear her trill, holding the moment:

a large café window awash with October sunshine,
splutter of leaves outside, hiss of breakfast fat inside,

while all the men turn from their mugs of steaming tea,
fix their eyes on the curve of her body

ruffled in polka-dot, the questioning pout of her lips,
as the Polish waitress explains with slow patience

what is contained inside a 'bubble & squeak'.
Then she'd sit down to order her first taste of it,

then another, then later maybe the Big Tracey's lunch.
And she'd come back every day so they'd know her order

as she walked in the door: *Bubble for Marilyn!*
So she'd grow fat and happy, sell the flyaway white car, stay.

Orkney Shell

I knew the name of it once
in my list-making days –
'common shell found on the northern coastline of Britain',
some such descriptor.

A kind of whelk I think,
dragged in by kind currents, deep sea swell,
chipped and broken, worn away.
But now I like it nameless –

a white, spiral sculpture
to fit in the palm of my hand,
more space than structure, more air than matter.
A thing that made itself

out of wind and water,
seasons of exposure.
My grandfather, my great-grandfather,
might have picked up one of these,

fingered it, pocketed it, homed it to darkness
and a little world of warm.
They would have known for sure
the salt corrosion of bitter air, the never-ending

hurl and hurry of wind.
Expected cruelty.
They would have known the very act of surviving.
And how it is passed on –

though we almost never know it till moments like these –
the wind blowing through us,
broken, gap-filled,
sadder and strong.

Family Tree

There's a preponderance of Jameses:
my father, his uncle (just born
then a question mark, as if he'd never lasted
beyond a breath, waited to see

what the world would be). Then
a sequence of gaps, lines that give out,
then another James, a great-great grandfather,
who'd married an Isabella in 1864,
on a distant Orkney island.
Her maiden name Groundwater,
like a small shiny stream. Domestic servant

marrying seaman, becoming seaman's wife,
to make more seamen, more wives and daughters,
one shopman, one scholar
till the schooling ran out.

At the top is George – very un-Scottish –
from the Isle of Westray (further Orkney).
Then a couple more Georges, stepping centuries
like uncertain stones, heavy with their names
on their seaman's backs,

marrying an Agnes in 1789,
espousing a Barbara (so outlandish a name) in 1845 –
one son John who was born
but never died. No date, no record,
and the same for many.
Still waiting to finish, to rest somewhere,

in between centuries, islands, water.
Just the last few moderns
who know their place, who end it all neatly
with a bracket round their dates.
Dead in 2003 is my schoolteacher mother,
correct and timely to the last,

while Agnes and Jessie, Christina and Maud
live on in the unknown
watching younger brothers leave on the tide,
tipping right over the edge of the world.
George goes to Canada –

where Ronald and Dorothy are placed
and grown. At the bottom of the page,
in an English suburb, I am almost watching them.
Dangling in space, my twin at my side,
my small hands reach out to them,
for they seem so close.
Just an inch of white paper

to be where they are. Just a short distance more,
unfathomable more,
to be George on his island, his treeless sky,
where he can see his Agnes
come walking towards him –
her slow steps printing the long white sand.

Island Stories

Somebody always begins by telling you
how they came for a day...

stayed. Another has colour-coded beehives
in a strip of garden, talks more to bees

than people, a perpetual whirr of wings
about his face, a hand to brush away

conversation. One brings cherries hard as bullets,
tomatoes, turnips, potatoes with old men's faces.

Another, glassy-eyed fish that watch you
baleful from the kitchen table.

Another grows nothing – in this land fit for no-one,
except dogs and drunks and geriatrics.

Everyone talks of weather, weather, weather –
days of fog, the sea snow, the sun,

the trees that gave up and the things that fell
in rain. *But never whisky* someone always jokes,

with a constancy of punchlines.
Just like the children who don't return,

the impassable days when the island shrinks
and you hate the taste of salt.

Occasionally some incomer talks of sky,
of space and freedom using too many words.

And somebody always ends by telling you
how they've wasted their time here,

how there was another life on land.
That perpetual sensation of something

forgotten – a bag of sugar, candles,
the batteries for a clock.

Verdigris

for Catherine Walston

I could weather shipwreck,
like Shakespeare's comic lovers.
Or find an unknown location – *What country friends is this?*
It's somewhere with a forest, a desert, a mountain.

It's a place I've never been,
and the trick for you would be to travel the world
until eventually you found me –
that should take some decades.

To extend the obstacle,
I'd of course be in disguise: man, woman, dog –
there's no second guessing.
Or maybe a blind beggar, some timeless hermaphrodite,

at the gates of the very last city you visit.
White stick, money box, coins in my eyes.
When you finally recognised me,
I'd drop the coins like a shot from my lids –

to locate those musicians
who've been waiting years
for comic resolution. *Strike up pipers! Music ho!*
Oh, it would be worth the waiting

for love to last this long…
even now I anticipate
the trace of your lips on my verdigrised eyelids,
your hands' slow unbuttoning

of my street-dusted clothes,
and the way you would say to me, as I began to recount
our obstacle-ridden story:
Peace, I will stop thy mouth (with a kiss).

Emails from Roberto

You write to tell me you are bicycling
through the fog. *This is the time of year
that depresses. Summer was different —*

what to do with my days now?
And I see you rimed with wet: cold fingers
on the handlebars, your breath like fog

inside the fog. Lost as you ever were,
you go cycling round your small town.
You write to tell me the weather, the years,

the place where I knew you, the windows
of your room that open onto the square,
the sun that is fogbound, the afternoons

that are almost evenings so you wheel your bike
down a darkening alley and walk right past
your very own door. And you write to tell me

that once you looked back and saw your flat window,
its brightly lit picture, hanging there in the foggy air —
a table, chair, a bowl of apples, warm blur

of curtain against the glass. How it looked
like the life, the easy-roomed happiness
of somebody else, and you cycled away.

Waiting to go on stage at 7.45pm on a windy March evening, and wondering why I do it

In the manner of James Wright
who writes titles like these,

who writes doors and windows too
on long-distance bus journeys,
tracks back into time,
who wanders in a foreign country
and notices the squint of maple leaves,
the good darkness of hands,
a bird half there and gone; the little things
that fix him for even a moment
in this unknowing of place, so he thinks –

this is existence, this is here and now:
a cup of coffee warming my hands,
the 6 am shadow becoming light,
slow click up my back of bone on bone;
so he stands as if for the first time
tall and complete, saying the words *I know;*

and here am I waiting to go on stage,
with James Wright beside me:
'*I know,*' he tells me, *will begin*
when you walk through that painted door;
into the roar of faces, the light,
into that strange home which is your story;
but there are oceans, wheatfields,
mudflats, beaches, dust tracks, roads
before I reach that door;
there are old coats, new trousers,
the fumble of buttons, uncertainty of zips,
last night's dream of nakedness,

my own voice waiting in the wordless dark,
and there are all the years of doing this....

Voice

I lock it in a box, and drop it here
at the corner of this beach:
a stretch of scruffy sand, swimmers
all gone, one solitary dog walker snapping sticks
into the wind.
Then I sit here and listen –

my voice in a box sounds different
from here, outside of me and bobbing
on the choppy waves,
sounds thinner, stranger,
out of its element.
But mostly I like the way I forget it, sometimes for hours,

so I hear only waves,
bringing other people's lives to this edge
of sand. A clank of a bottle;
an old shirt's flailing arms;
rope, old rope; one battered shoe, laceless, open,
in a tangle of bladderwrack.

Or sometimes there's just silence,
and I like that too.
The feeling inside it that I could begin
with a new voice all over again.
Every one of my words,
salty, rinsed and glittering.

Summer Pudding

in memory of Adriana Caudrey

Easy to make it. I wake up in November,
years after, and hear your voice saying it
with a strange authority for a girl who can't cook.

White bread, the cheapest. Strawberries,
raspberries, blackcurrants... Tart summer fruits.
So soon we are de-crusting Mother's Pride White,

lining the bowl in strips, then boiling up red fruits,
black fruits, blue. Then pouring them over,
a slow syrup river,

then more layers of bread, more river, more bread.
I upside down it, sit it resplendent
on a wide white plate –

summer mountain.
We eat it up quickly, raspberry seeds
like grit between our teeth.

You skim your plate with a finger,
the way you once did with cake crumbs
when a student, lick the last of it,

still talking, laughing, eating,
swinging a bag, leaving. Awkward at doorways.
And we can't waste what's left us...

Fruits. Summer. River. Mountain.
Blue, black, red. Any colour. All of it.
We can't waste a second of what you have left us.

South America Poems

Fleeting Considerations

We remind voyagers
that they should leave precious objects
in a case of security at reception.
Please take this precaution with gentleness.
We salute and thank you. The Direction.

Found poem: reception sign at Hotel Puerto Valparaiso, Chile

Where I've Been

Come close and I'll tell you
the story of it. Words for glacier, canyon, desert,
monuments of my travelling time.

Come closer if you still can't believe...
I'll breathe blue and white, mud brown and
dry yellow. You've never felt colours
like these on your cheek, inside your ear.

What still no belief? Come even closer,
you shall have my body, print your hands over
all the flesh of me – everything undone,
and truth for the touching.

Do you know now where I've been,
how strange it was and how familiar you seemed
from that far away?

To My New Karrimor Walking Boots

You should be tried, you should be worn,
not these pristine unscuffed, black toes,
these perfect plaits of laces, the neat,
clean under-ridges on your soles.
At the very least, you should have walked
a few London streets, a few Surrey lanes,
splashed mud on your surfaces,
become some imprint of who I am now.
Bone, muscle, nail – any of it.
But you resisted, didn't you?
Sat in your box for at least a week,
waiting for this space, this pilgrim distance.
Now you rock a little for beginnings,
test surfaces for the knowing, anticipate –
how toes are spread inside you,
then you begin to walk. Walk.
There is all this earth to print on, pace over.
There is memory of muscle
that comes in your sleep, when I count the steps
backwards. Walk, walk, walk.
There is distance that leaves its mark
in your broken black ridges, your creased,
splattered sides, your new-worn hollows.
Now, and now, I'll put my hands inside you
and feel all your walking. Write it, sing it.
There is nothing truer than what you tell me.
All journeys are forgetfulness,
or an act of trying too hard to remember,
but look at you, new Karrimor boots,
now old, you are here to tell me simply
this is where I've been.

Tango

I go backwards into love,
    foot behind. I lean into nights
full of the old world:

ship ballast, squid, a bleeding Christ,
    Virgin like a doll,
or simply the one candle

of what I wanted to believe.
    Then I pause, as this room
pauses, drinkers held in mirror glass,

an oversweet taste on the tongue,
    in the mouth, and all the things
I might have done

hang glittering in the air,
    a hovering chandelier.
You are against me, you are

gone. I lean forwards into space:
    open windows, night,
somewhere the never-ending line

of grass, the tomorrows of rain.
    Then I go backwards into love,
foot behind.

Café San Pedro, Buenos Aires

It's too late now to tell you:
this street, this café, this worn, hooped chair,
its yellow paint flecked to red, to brown;
all that patina.
And this beer the *padrona* serves me,
its prickle in my throat – what I wanted, what I got,

and how on days like this
it makes me lightheaded.
And to add for you the picture of her:
old mascara eyes, wide lipstick smile,
a lopsided chignon streaked blond, streaked grey;
the way she has of owning her world,
this small green café –

how I sit and feel welcomed.
Then to enumerate the place, detail by detail:
the photo of Evita perched on the cash till,
the cook's old bicycle parked behind the bar,
just this day or every day? And to comment to you
how routine can be effortful,

but perhaps he freewheels home?
Then to count the lunchtime diners in, one by one:
well-dressed mamma's boys
in white shirts and ties,
a man in a brown suit and an under-the-table-dog,
woman with magazine not eating, not drinking.
And now to point out the blind lady

entering the café this very moment,
paused in the doorway, her hands outstretched,
then guided by her son to a safe island table –
how this simple action makes the café
stop: forks paused, beers raised,
the song on the radio swelling the silence;

makes everything ordinary
for a second significant.
How love can do that,
you feel it and know it.
But it's too late, late now to tell you.

Gardel

*In June 1935, a Cuban woman committed suicide in Havana,
and a woman in New York and another in Puerto Rico tried to
poison themselves, all over the death of the same man, the singer
Carlos Gardel – whom none of them had ever met.*

I slice onions and think of him.
I peel the red peppers and lay them in oil,
cut them into letter-shaped days. I post them
into my husband's unsmiling mouth.

I type the pages and think of him.
I beat them like a drum on my Bluebird typewriter
through the songless hours. I lay them
on the director's desk, its mahogany mirror.

I take the bird out of its singing cage
and think of him. I smooth its feathers
against the dark. Then I swallow its silence
all the way down to the bottom of the bottle.

The Glacier's Song

I am there behind you.
A long white shadow
at your turning back.
A silence bigger

than all your little noise.
Your toast is burnt,
your tea is cold.
The bus runs late

on the London road.
And your bicycle wheels
can never turn fast enough.
I am there behind you.

At night the heating
ticks and ticks to a pavement cold.
It's still too warm.
So write your name

on a dust-covered car.
Delete your photos
till the picture fits,
your teeth as white as they can be.

Now smile in the dark,
hold him closer, closer
in your little forever.
I am there behind you.

Market

This holding up, this spreading out.
Damp fennel on my fingers, the shine of apple,
and rows of lemons pinched and proud –

already they tingle acid at my tongue.
Can I buy anticipation? The flap of awning,
lazy crab claw, antenna waving behind the glass,

and fish in piles, strings of eels. Fling a bucket
over all their death, shine a shop window.
Can I look inside to remember now not then?

Go deeper, there's the darkness of cool,
the hard rub of smell: salt and blood, one animal eye
somewhere watching, while the dogs at the entrance

bark their way to a leftover Sunday. Water
down the drain, what's left, what's used.
Did I keep what I meant to?

Walk the gallery dark: there's an artichoke heart,
there are cabbages as roses in disguise,
and flowers in pails that light the pavement.

Can I hold them against me in the crush of traffic?
Will I kill their light? A bird is lost
in all this glass – I can hear its heart rising up, up, up.

A fish, a daffodil, something forgotten.
The smell of everything is on my hands.
And did I find what I wished for? Did I?

Oblivion

after the music of Astor Piazzolla, Buenos Aires

Don't come here. It's an old place.
The cakes are stale and stiff with sugar.
Fast-slow, fast-slow coda, I am locked in it.

The coffee will keep you awake all night
till sleep is something you barely remember.
Don't come here. It's an old place.

The double bass gives a believable depth,
that bandeon a flight of lyricism.
Fast-slow, fast-slow coda, I am locked in it.

But he plays the piano as if he hated it, loved it,
felt only indifference. I watch him in the silvered mirror.
Don't come here. It's an old place.

Didn't they tell you at the door
in the half-light, as you paid your way in?
Fast-slow, fast-slow coda, I am locked in it.

I know, I came here, though they gave me
land and space and days of everywhere.
Don't come here. It's an old place.
Fast-slow, fast-slow coda, I am locked in it.

Man with Dogs

Bariloche, Argentina

They follow me everywhere in this unknown place –
sleepy dogs, fast dogs, the flea-bitten and one-eyed –

here they come, loping and shambling behind me.
Along the beach too, over rocks and slippery lichen,

through the dead trees that stand shocked and white
out in the fields, come silent dogs, soulful dogs.

In the streets, they pad at my side,
past dazed and closed afternoon shops,

right up the steps of the long, steep garden
to my rented house overlooking the bay.

Now the red one, the black and white one,
to rub themselves at the backs of my legs, place their whole heads

inside my cupped hand, snuffle a wet nose further in.
Almost as if it were some conspiracy: make the stranger

stay, stay. Then at night, when I look out of my window,
they gather there beneath the ledge, look a dark brown eye

up at me, pant their sides, wait. In the morning,
there at my door, they begin again.

The short, scruffy one, the other with a vigorous tail.
And later, when I see myself in the town shop windows,

I almost believe in what I see: legs, paws moving
in perfect synchronicity, noses pointed in the same direction.

There he goes, they seem to say, that man with his dogs,
going somewhere he knows very fast.

Cities

after Julian Stannard

Cities you don't want to arrive at in the night.
Cities of breathlessness, and rain on the voodoo heads hanging
      in side alleys.
Cities of walking, the hard pattern and print of too many
      pavement slabs, boulevards big enough for Paris.
Cities of small victories: Sally with her six new pairs of shoes,
      in pastel colours she can't get in London.
Cities of crooks, traitors and killers, all the next cities are cities of killers:
      Don't get into a taxi, they cut you in pieces, dump you in a river.
      I knew someone who knew someone… says Kari the Swedish girl.
Cities of stopping, the sweetness of cakes, *dulce de leche*,
      a window that frames your own volcano.
Cities of nuns, then cities of penguins.
Cities of religion, the blood congealed, the fingers in the blood,
      but Jesus has real hair just like Gloria Gaynor.
Cities of waiting and the smell of bad fish.
Cities the buses don't stop in.
Cities of vastness, and Robin will meet me in the main plaza on his way
      back from Patagonia, but it is vast and when I walk to
      one corner he may be at the other.
Cities of no mobile connection.
Cities talked about for days and never arrived at.
Cities of emptiness, when the need for nitrates ran out:
      no more orders from England, no more letters home.
Cities of sunstroke.
Cities of tiny bowler hats balanced precariously on the tops
      of women's heads, impossible hats I follow all the way
      down the street.
Cities of colours that don't/shouldn't go, all pink and orange.
Cities of ice where I can't hire a bicycle.
Cities of sex where I go looking for you the next night, find you –
      incredibly in all these people, but you don't want to talk to me.
Cities of Neruda, no news, nothing more to say.
Cities of mud and spotless white serviettes.
Cities of chicken wings, sticky rice and pizza.
Cities of meat and superlatives, a swimming pool at the top
      of a luxury hotel where Linda will shoot her film about tango
      but only if she can find enough unpaid extras.

Robinson

Isla Crusoe, Chile

To tell the truth, I wanted off that island as soon as the boat
turned its sail in the bay. My own sheer arrogance,
my argumentative turn of phrase, and look at the result:
two long years and four and a half months of loneliness
with myself. I shouted and shouted, but that bastard boat
sailed on and left me. So I was king of nowhere, emperor
of almost nothing. Seven square miles, fourteen banana trees
(I counted them all), a scribble of wild maize
and prickly cactus. And for company just the lollop of seals,
their salty whiskers, their know-it-all eyes, like drunkards
who were too far gone to be bothered even to bore you
with their story of how, where, why. For there was
no answer. And no Man Friday either, no bloody footprint
in the sand, no hours and hours of attempted understanding.
Just myself, myself, the sun by day, the freezing nights,
the need for survival, then the need for a reason why.
And my own voice defaulting, my own voice giving up,
and with it the edges of everything I was. Yes,
there were scraps of prayers, half-hymns in the memory;
there were lost routines, the odd word of harshness,
even the odd word of praise which lingered for a while,
until they burned at the corners, drowned in salt water.
Then almost nothing at all. Just a voice inside my head,
the echo in its corners. I remind myself sometimes
I was never more than this, after all that walking on the earth.
And by the way, it was never Robinson. Alexander's the name.

My Motorcycle Diaries or Travelling with Robin

You are the diver
at the shores of this lake where we have our small *cabaña*,
our two-day house off the road to nowhere,
between Chile and Argentina.
You are the one who strips, cuts

straight into the blue, bobs a cool head along the surface,
shakes yourself like a dog, then demands warm,
demands food, demands shade.
You are not this bundle of clothes and too many books
stuffed into a motorbike pannier
at the eleventh hour,

the phut phut phut of the bike
as it clings to the road going up the hill,
nor the rider who looks forwards, backwards,
who wonders if he should have stayed,
been the one on the shore,

the one cutting clearly into the blue,
the other one, or all those other ones
who write, rewrite their lives,
keeping themselves awake in some other *cabaña*
while the motorbike engine
ticks to cool outside.

Encounters on the Road to Machu Picchu

Tia is here on her way to Cuba. We trek for two days:
her white-blond hair in all that green.

I can't bear the darkness in Sweden. She's twenty.
What should I do with my life? France and Francis

have it all sorted: marriage, a house in the Montreal suburbs.
I will mend bicycles, broken skis. In the morning airport,

they open their bag packed with presents for the family:
llama socks, llama caps, handmade oven gloves (llama design).

Carlotta tells me *You're not like the usual tourists I get.*
She shows me the nunnery, speaking grills for the family/

the novices; the small cakes they bake, bright blue cloister walls.
Like the colour of your eyes. Englishman you blush. I look away.

To Berndt at my side: his cycling vest, the buttons of his nipples.
We are walking up a canyon, the sweat down his vest

in a long dark line. *I like practising my English.* I like watching his
half-smile.
Alejandro's in love with a lazy Australian. Stuck in a traffic jam

somewhere in the desert, he tells me in the darkness
We met in Edinburgh, my family don't know that I am gay.

Australia, he weeps, *it is so far away.* Where Nicole and Paul
are building a new house: internet updates, the neighbours in dispute.

She draws me the rooms on a paper tablecloth, in between
bus stations. *This is our bedroom with a view of the bay.*

Francesco's is windowless – he slips me in past the dozing concierge.
We undress in the half light, though I can see the hair all over his
chest.

A slim Italian architect, he will build houses in Rome.
Tomorrow I leave to climb mountains. I should sleep.

He should collect the clothes scattered round the room.
On a late night train, Seamus confides *I had to leave Ireland,*

tells me proudly how he drank his way round South America.
Some countries you know, I don't even remember.

The Young

They're on their way to Byzantium
with everything in their pocket.
There's no forgetfulness, no curtain falling
behind them. They text, they phone,

they email. They carry their world with them,
neat and shiny as a tiny light. They travel this globe
so knowingly. But I went to Byzantium
with a kind of unknowing in my eye.

I forgot the place I came from, never spoke to it
or wrote. I was in the dark with another language
in my mouth, and the lights of Byzantium
glowed through all my unsleeping.

Tomorrow, I thought, I'd stand in the square,
in Ecuador, India, any Byzantium.
I'd tell myself what I understood
and the dark would answer me.

Last Supper with a Guinea Pig

after the painting by Marcos Zapata, 18th century, Cuzco Cathedral

Jesus is really above it all at this point,
holding the bread symbolically, only symbolically,
his mind intent on the next chapter of the story,
eyes already heavenward, his halo visibly brightening.

The disciples on his side are all begging him to eat,
But the baskets of food remain untouched,
even the just-ripe mangos, bulging figs,
the fragrant Peruvian cheeses cut neatly in ready triangles.

On the other side, they are fidgetting...
one looking our way, scratching his beard;
another gesturing impotent, all this good food going to waste;
the one to the right on the point of leaving.

While the other on the left
has his eyes on that guinea pig, that lean, longed-for flesh,
that savour of roast tingling in his nostrils:
everything he's ever wanted.

This evening, Jesus, we have guinea pig,
the best dish in Peru, please don't preach abstinence,
not on this special guinea pig evening,
Mr Left disciple whispers almost tearfully.

Well, the aftermath we all know.
The bread, the wine, the betrayal of morning.
But not what happened to that guinea pig,
which waits, legs poised in candle-lit mid air.

Did no-one eat it? Or did one of those disciples
(Mr Left?) creep back later after that foodless supper
and wrap it carefully in a leftover napkin,
persuading himself as we humans do

that the absolute sacrifice was all very well,
but belief has its place
and you need some sustenance – a little packed lunch? –
for such a long, hard journey.

The Drifter in the Blue Houses

after Tu Mu, 803-852

These houses are all rain.
I am clicking through weather forecasts,
country by country: I want sun,
just a little sun, I am glued to the screen.

Hope is an icon. Click here.
I am naked in the sauna, my nipples hard
and ready. I want your shadow at the door,
I want. Hope is in my mouth, my tongue

will find it out. This is why I travel –
a drifter in the blue houses, the one
who eats late and sleeps all morning;
finds out what he doesn't know;

who checks a face in that uncertain mirror,
breaks in shoes on unfamiliar pavements.
Snake-blue leather, pointed toes,
they click and echo as I pass.

Whale Watching

Puerto Lopez, Ecuador

But the whales will not come: no blue-grey shadow,
no sudden water blow across my horizon. I am

too early, too late; the water current not quite the right
temperature; or it's global warming, it's someone else's

fault. But 'tours abandoned' says the dangling sign
on the Ecuatours door, written inside the outline

of a smiling whale. And I'm stalled in this seaside town,
in an expensive hotel room, with nothing to do.

I am emailing you – whom I have never met but almost
love, the words go so deep: each day a nudge more

into feeling across my dark computer screen.
And those whales boom slowly through my uncertain sleep...

I go following their radar, the electric blue lines,
am nearly at the surface of something new.

I am pursing my lips, holding my breath – almost
in spite of myself, I could believe, could follow. Here I go.

Hammock

for Neil on his 50th Birthday

I choose it carefully, its reds, purples, yellows –
strong colours you might use for one of your paintings –
stripe on stripe, hanging from the market stall.

I test its handles, plaited, multi-coloured,
loops that will hold through time and time.
Then I carry it with me from place to place

on my South American journey; cargo it with stories
on buses, trains, down long, dusty roads.
All the weight of new things. But mostly I carry it

here in my head – already suspended in your Oxford garden –
balanced, held, above that wilderness
of bushes, flowers, tumbling greenery, the heads and arms

of lichened statuary, one tall brick wall.
And already you're floating in its reds, purples, yellows,
confidently held in one broad brushstroke –

such a practised hand, such a labour of courage,
the penniless years, the almost falling,≥ still believing –
in this mellow afternoon, in this everywhere of light.

Goodbye

I get good at going,
sizing up a town, a city, a village,
by the quick scan of a map,

sniffing out bargain beds, *menus del día,*
playing the poor traveller
in spite of my shiny new suitcase on wheels,
my pocketful of dollars,

and leaving, leaving.
And yes, I cream off memories –
cock crow, blue light, an island in a lake,
bundles wrapped in striped cloth,
saints with real hair,
monkey call, mud,
the lidless eye of a crocodile.
But I get so good at going –

I am gone before I'm there,
have written the anticipation, have traded
the farewell. Before the goodbye
is even on your lips –

faces, doorways, streets, cathedrals,
factories, mines, your piece of sky,
I am in another country,

I am early for tomorrow. Please wake me
if I arrive.

Ulysses in South America

He's always there,
riding the bus for instance up the motorway
of Chile, rain sluicing the window

while the women queue at every station stop
to sell him *empanadas*, fish, packages of underwear.
Suits you sir, they say, eyeing him up,

and pressing the boxers, tangas, multi-coloured slips
into his lap. He resists them this time,
has his own small music plugged in his ears,

keeps going away, going,
trying to get back. Somewhere in between.
On a different bus – was it in Ecuador? –

somebody stands to preach the way of the Lord,
a tiny boy sells bootleg DVDs.
Ulysses sleeps through it: religion's too familiar,

and the DVD films all reduce, he knows,
to six basic stories.
Surely he is one of them? Bolivia next,

and he paces the glaring whiteness of salt flat,
a texture like time crumbling under his feet,
or walks the desert into the blackest of nights.

This is more like it – something endless,
something blinding he thinks. Or forgetfulness
that might be a sort of new beginning.

Somewhere to go.
Tricked again! mutters Ulysses, pitching up early
at the morning bus station – was it Peru? –

old suitcases, new labels,
and another bus ride to rock and lull him.
He'll let some other traveller

nudge a head against his shoulder:
going away, gone... Plug his own small music
into his ears, till the batteries fail.

Acknowledgements

'21 Ways of Starting a New Life' was commended in the Scintilla 12 competition.

'O' was commended in the Yorkshire poetry competition.

'Pip' and 'Summer Pudding' were commended in Wells Festival poetry competition.

With special thanks to the Thursday Group, and especially Jane Duran, for their continued inspiration and support.